A **TRUE** BOOK™

RESPIRATORY SYSTEM

Cody Crane

Children's Press®
An imprint of Scholastic Inc.

T0027325

Content Consultant
Tom Johnson
Former Director, Respiratory Care, Long Island University
Professor of Cardiopulmonary Medicine

Copyright © 2024 by Scholastic Inc.
All rights reserved. Published by Children's Press, an imprint of Scholastic Inc., *Publishers since 1920*. SCHOLASTIC, CHILDREN'S PRESS, A TRUE BOOK™, and associated logos are trademarks and/or registered trademarks of Scholastic Inc.

The publisher does not have any control over and does not assume any responsibility for author or third-party websites or their content.

No part of this publication may be reproduced, stored in a retrieval system, or transmitted in any form or by any means, electronic, mechanical, photocopying, recording, or otherwise, without written permission of the publisher. For information regarding permission, write to Scholastic Inc., Attention: Permissions Department, 557 Broadway, New York, NY 10012.

Library of Congress Cataloging-in-Publication Data available
ISBN 978-1-339-02096-9 (library binding) | ISBN 978-1-339-02097-6 (paperback)

10 9 8 7 6 5 4 3 2 1   24 25 26 27 28

Printed in China 62
First edition, 2024

Design by Kathleen Petelinsek
Series produced by Spooky Cheetah Press

Find the Truth!

Everything you are about to read is true *except* for one of the sentences on this page.

Which one is **TRUE**?

T or F   The heart is part of the body's respiratory system.

T or F   A sneeze happens when unwanted particles get into your nose.

Find the answers in this book.

What's in This Book?

The BIG Truth

These tiny air sacs are inside your lungs.

Teamwork!

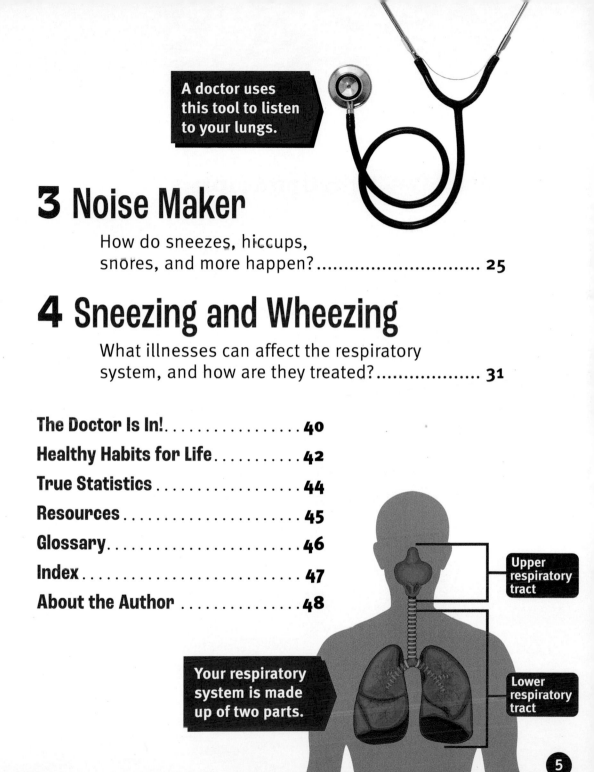

A doctor uses this tool to listen to your lungs.

3 Noise Maker

How do sneezes, hiccups, snores, and more happen?

4 Sneezing and Wheezing

What illnesses can affect the respiratory system, and how are they treated?

Your respiratory system is made up of two parts.

Upper respiratory tract

Lower respiratory tract

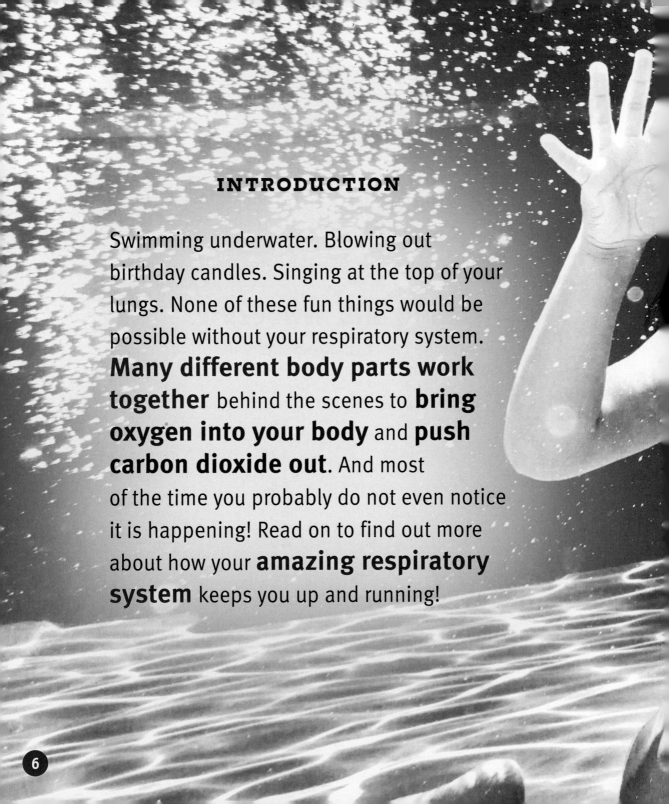

INTRODUCTION

Swimming underwater. Blowing out birthday candles. Singing at the top of your lungs. None of these fun things would be possible without your respiratory system. **Many different body parts work together** behind the scenes to **bring oxygen into your body** and **push carbon dioxide out**. And most of the time you probably do not even notice it is happening! Read on to find out more about how your **amazing respiratory system** keeps you up and running!

A person breathes in and out about 17,000 times a day! Our breathing rate varies based on our oxygen needs.

The average person can safely hold their breath for one to two minutes.

People breathe in through one side of their nose more than the other.

You breathe in more than 2,000 gallons of air each day!

Go with the Flow

Your respiratory system is divided into two parts. The first section is called the upper respiratory tract. It is made up of your nose, mouth, throat, and larynx [LAR-ingks]. These body parts move air into your lungs. Air usually enters your body through your nose. But if your nose is stuffed up, or if you are running fast, air can also enter through your mouth.

Take a Sniff

When you breathe in, air travels into your nostrils, where it is warmed up and moistened. Your nostrils are the two holes in your nose. The insides of your nostrils are lined with tiny hairs and **mucus**. The hairs and mucus trap dust and germs that could hurt your lungs or make you sick. Your nose also has another important job. It gives you your sense of smell. Inside your nose are special **cells**. They detect different scents.

Your nose contains millions of scent-detecting cells.

The mouth is also responsible for talking, chewing, tasting, and swallowing.

You swallow up to 1,000 times a day!

Say "Ahhh!"

The back of the nose and mouth connect to the throat, which is also known as the pharynx [FAIR-ingks]. There, the throat splits into two passages. One is called the esophagus [i-SAH-fuh-guhs]. It carries food and drinks from your mouth to your stomach. The other passage is the larynx. Air moves through this hollow **organ** on its way to your lungs.

Open and Shut

At the top of the larynx is a flap of tissue called the epiglottis [ep-uh-GLAH-tuhs]. When you swallow, the flap closes over the larynx. That keeps food and liquid out. Food can accidentally get into the larynx if you talk or laugh while eating. That can cause you to choke. Usually, when that happens, you cough until air from the lungs forces the food out. Then you can breathe properly again.

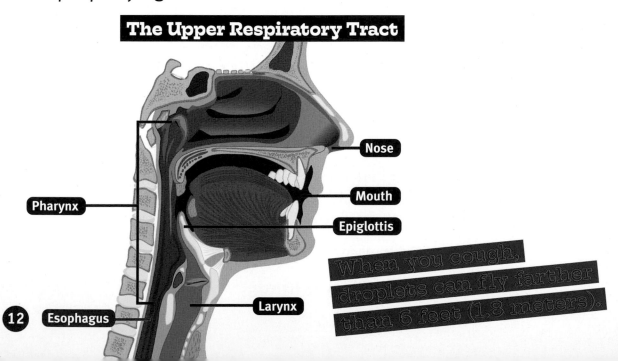

The Upper Respiratory Tract

Nose

Mouth

Epiglottis

Pharynx

Larynx

Esophagus

When you cough, droplets can fly farther than 6 feet (1.8 meters).

Chatterbox

The larynx has another important job. It helps you talk! This organ, also called the voice box, is where your vocal cords are found. They are two bands of smooth muscle that lie on either side of the larynx. Here is how your vocal cords work.

Open vocal cords

Larynx

Closed vocal cords

1 Vocal cords normally remain open to allow air to pass into the lungs.

2 When you speak, your vocal cords come together. The vocal cords vibrate as air passes through the tiny space between them.

3 The vibration of the vocal cords creates sound. Your mouth, tongue, and lips shape the sound into words.

Your lungs work a lot like balloons, filling with air and then partially deflating.

Fill 'er Up

The lower respiratory tract is the second part of the respiratory system. It is made up of the trachea [TRAY-kee-uh], bronchi [BRAHNG-kye], and lungs. The trachea and bronchi are tubes that carry air to your lungs. Your lungs are a pair of organs in your chest. Every time you breathe in, your lungs expand as they fill with air. When you breathe out, they contract, or shrink.

Your left lung is slightly smaller than your right to leave room for your heart.

Wind Tunnel

After air passes through the larynx, it flows into the trachea. The trachea is also known as the windpipe. It is a hollow tube that is made up of C-shaped rings of cartilage. This stiff tissue is also found in the outside of your ears and the tip of your nose. It is what makes them firm, yet squishy. The cartilage rings support the trachea, while also allowing it to flex. The trachea extends through the neck.

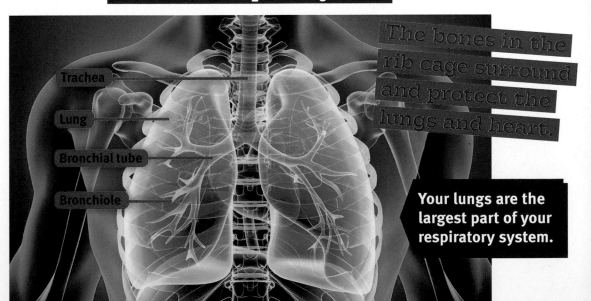

The Lower Respiratory Tract

Trachea

Lung

Bronchial tube

Bronchiole

The bones in the rib cage surround and protect the lungs and heart.

Your lungs are the largest part of your respiratory system.

This is what cilia look like under a microscope.

Branching Out

The trachea splits into two branches called the bronchial tubes. One connects to the right lung. The other connects to the left lung. Both the trachea and bronchial tubes are lined with cells. They are covered in mucus and tiny hairlike structures called **cilia**. The cilia move back and forth. They sweep mucus, and anything trapped in it, up to the throat. You then swallow, cough, or blow your nose to remove the gunk from your airways.

Acids in your stomach will quickly dissolve swallowed mucus—and any germs trapped there.

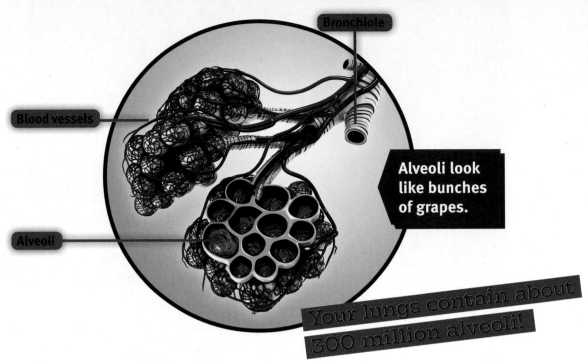

Bronchiole

Blood vessels

Alveoli

Alveoli look like bunches of grapes.

Your lungs contain about 300 million alveoli!

Oxygen Goes In . . .

The bronchial tubes keep dividing inside your lungs. They form smaller and smaller tubes called bronchioles. At the end of each bronchiole are air sacs called **alveoli** that are surrounded by tiny **blood vessels**. The oxygen in the air passes through the alveoli into the blood vessels beyond. The oxygen latches on to red blood cells inside the vessels and is carried to cells all over the body.

. . . Waste Goes Out

The body's cells use oxygen to make energy so they can function. Without oxygen, you could not move your muscles, digest food, or even think! As cells work, they make carbon dioxide as waste. Your blood picks up this gas waste and carries it to the lungs. There, carbon dioxide passes from blood vessels into the lung's alveoli. When you breathe out, carbon dioxide is pushed up the bronchial tubes and trachea. Then it flows out through your nose and mouth.

The trachea has between 16 and 20 rings.

Gently run your hand down the front of your neck. You can feel your trachea and its rings of cartilage.

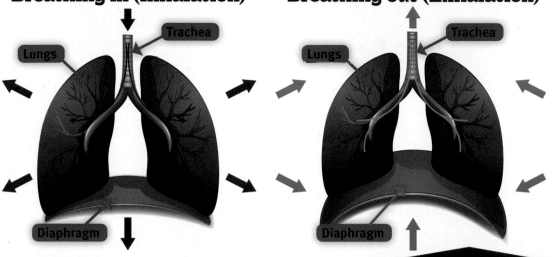

Breathing in (Inhalation)

Trachea

Lungs

Diaphragm

Breathing out (Exhalation)

Trachea

Lungs

Diaphragm

Moving Muscles

When your diaphragm moves down, your lungs expand. When it moves up, your lungs deflate.

The diaphragm [DYE-uh-fram] is a curved muscle below the lungs. When you breathe in, this muscle moves down and flattens. Muscles between your rib cage also push your chest out. It creates a suction that causes the lungs to expand, drawing air into your body. When you breathe out, the diaphragm and rib muscles relax. This causes the lungs to partially deflate. Air inside gets squeezed out of your body. Your brain controls the muscles involved in breathing, and you don't even have to think about it.

What Is Air?

You cannot see it, taste it, or smell it. But air is all around us. Air is a mix of gases. They form Earth's atmosphere, which covers the planet like a blanket. Most living things need some of the gases in the air. Many creatures, including humans, need oxygen to live. This gas makes up 21 percent of the atmosphere. Carbon dioxide, which we breathe out as waste, makes up a much smaller portion of the atmosphere: 0.04 percent.

Gases That Make Up Earth's Atmosphere

Nitrogen
78%

Oxygen
21%

0.9%   Argon
0.04% Carbon dioxide
0.06% Other

21

Teamwork!

The respiratory system does not function on its own. Find out how it works with other systems in your body to keep you running!

Muscular System:

The movement of muscles in your chest pulls and pushes air into and out of your lungs. In turn, the respiratory system provides these hardworking muscles with oxygen to keep them going.

Circulatory System:

Every time your heart beats, it moves blood around the body. One of blood's most important jobs is to carry oxygen from the lungs to cells. It then returns carbon dioxide back to the lungs to be exhaled.

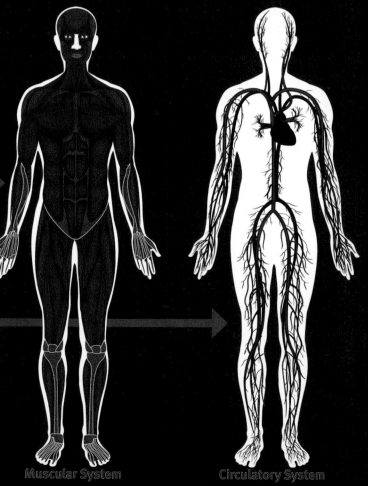

Muscular System

Circulatory System

Digestive System:

The cells that make up your digestive system need oxygen to do their job breaking down food. These nutrients then supply energy to fuel the respiratory system's cells.

Nervous System:

Your brain controls your breathing. It is connected to special sensory cells called nerves. They can sense the level of oxygen and carbon dioxide in the blood. When necessary, the nerves signal to your brain to speed up or slow down your breathing.

Skeletal System:

Your bones protect your body. Those in your skull protect your upper respiratory tract. The bones in your neck and chest protect your lower respiratory tract. Bones are made of living cells. They, in turn, need oxygen from the respiratory system to survive.

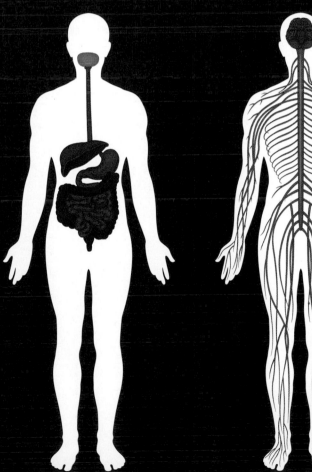

Digestive System

Nervous System

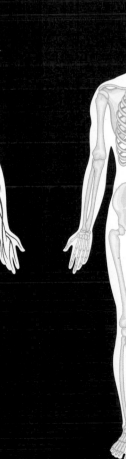

Skeletal System

Yawns are contagious.
If you see someone yawn,
you might yawn too.

When you
yawn, that's
your respiratory
system at work.

24

Noise Maker

Talking and coughing are two noisy things your respiratory system can do. But those are not the only sounds it makes. In fact, this system is behind most of the noises that come from your body—including sneezes, hiccups, and snores. Read on to find out about the different noises your respiratory system makes.

A sneeze can travel up to 100 miles (160 kilometers) per hour!

You don't sneeze when you are asleep because the nerves that cause sneezing are also asleep.

ACHOO!

A sneeze happens when unwanted particles like dust, germs, or smoke enter your nose. That triggers tiny hairs inside your nostrils, causing you to take in a sharp breath. Your eyes close tightly. Then your chest muscles quickly tighten. Air is forced from your lungs. Your tongue moves to the top of your mouth. That directs the blast of air out through your nose, getting rid of that annoying speck tickling it!

Are You Bored or Just Tired?

When you yawn, your mouth opens wide. You draw in a deep breath, which is followed by a short exhale. Yawning is a reflex. That means something causes It to happen without your control. Scientists are not sure what causes us to yawn. But it often happens when we are tired. So maybe it helps you breathe deeper to take in more oxygen to wake up your sleepy brain. People also yawn when they are bored. So maybe yawning is meant to signal to others how you are feeling.

Many animals yawn, including mammals, birds, fish, and reptiles.

HIC!

Hiccups happen when your diaphragm moves down suddenly over and over. The motion causes your body to suck in air and your vocal cords to snap shut. The result is a "hic" sound. It is not clear why people get hiccups. It might happen after you drink a bubbly drink. Or hiccups might happen because you eat or drink too fast. Luckily, they usually go away quickly.

Babies hiccup more than kids or adults.

Some people try to get rid of hiccups by holding their breath or drinking water quickly. But there is no proof these cures work.

Most snoring is about as loud as a person talking, making it hard for others to sleep.

Sound Asleep?

Nearly everyone snores sometimes. Your throat muscles relax when you sleep. Breathing can cause these relaxed muscles to vibrate, which creates a harsh buzzing sound. That is a snore. The more deeply asleep you are, the more likely you are to snore. That is also true if you are sleeping on your back or have a stuffy nose. Both of those things can block your airways slightly and lead to snoring.

Most kids get 6 to 10 colds a year!

More than 200 different viruses can cause the common cold.

Sneezing and Wheezing

Chances are you have had at least one cold in your life. You got sick because a **virus** infected your respiratory system. You likely got the virus on your hands, then touched your nose—and that's how the virus entered your body. It likely caused symptoms like sneezing, a sore throat, a runny nose, and a cough. A cold is just one illness that affects the respiratory system. Find out about some others, which all share one thing in common. They make it hard for people to breathe.

Feeling Sick

Like a cold, the flu is caused by a virus that infects the lungs. The flu shares many symptoms with a cold, but those symptoms are usually worse with the flu. Along with a runny nose and a cough, people with the flu can also suffer muscle aches, high fever, and vomiting. The flu can make elderly people, young children, and people with serious health conditions very sick. It can even be life-threatening.

Timeline: Milestones in Respiratory Medicine History

3000 BCE
An Egyptian text makes the first mention that the body contains lungs.

1816 CE
French doctor René Laënnec uses a paper tube to listen to a patient's chest. It is the first stethoscope.

1858
Dr. Henry Silvester publishes his method of creating artificial respiration by raising and lowering a patient's arms to make them draw in air.

1918–1919
The Spanish flu, a deadly new version of the disease, infects about one-third of the world's population.

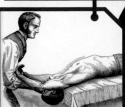

Serious Infection

Sometimes, a person's body has a hard time fighting off a virus like the flu. They can then develop a worse illness called pneumonia [noo-MOHN-yuh]. Some **bacteria** can also cause pneumonia. The disease causes the lung's alveoli to fill with fluid. The person then has a hard time breathing. Elderly people, infants, and people who already have another serious health condition are the most likely to get pneumonia.

EARLY 1940s
Thomas Francis and Jonas Salk develop the first flu **vaccine**.

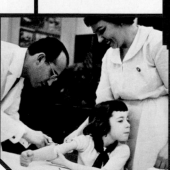

1960
Cardiopulmonary resuscitation (CPR) is improved. This emergency procedure can help a person who has stopped breathing.

1963
Dr. James Hardy performs the first lung transplant, replacing a patient's diseased lung with a healthy one from another person.

2021
A Covid-19 vaccine is made available to kids.

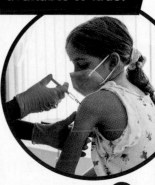

Up to 30 percent of the world's population suffers from seasonal allergies.

People who have allergies have to avoid the thing that makes them sick or take medicine.

Allergy Time

An allergic reaction happens when your **immune system** overreacts to something in the environment. In the case of seasonal allergies, the immune system is often reacting to pollen. At certain times of the year, many plants release pollen into the air so that new plants can grow. Symptoms of seasonal allergies include sneezing, coughing, and a runny nose.

Hard to Breathe

Asthma is an illness that causes the airways in the lungs to swell. As a result, the space inside the airways narrows. This leads to wheezing, shortness of breath, and a tight feeling in the chest. Things like exercise, cold air, pollution, and allergies can trigger a person's asthma. Some people have minor asthma symptoms that need only occasional treatment. But for others, asthma is a chronic disease that requires daily treatment with inhalers and other medications. An asthma attack can be serious and require emergency medical attention.

A device called an inhaler delivers medicine that helps quickly stop asthma symptoms.

Worldwide Virus

In 2019, a new respiratory virus began spreading around the globe. The virus caused an illness called Covid-19 that led to a **pandemic**. People suffered symptoms like coughing, shortness of breath, headache, tiredness, and even loss of taste and smell. Some people had mild cases. But for millions of others, Covid-19 was deadly. People wore masks, washed their hands often, and kept their distance from others. This, along with a vaccine, helped stop the spread of Covid-19.

During the pandemic, many kids attended school remotely over the internet.

Travel between many countries was halted during the Covid-19 pandemic.

WASH HANDS: Wash with soap and water for at least 20 seconds. Do this after you visit crowded areas or blow your nose and before you eat.

MASK UP: Wear a mask when you go out to a public place.

GET VACCINATED: Get vaccinated to reduce your chances of catching illnesses like the flu or suffering a serious case of Covid-19.

Stopping the Spread

Viruses that infect the respiratory system are usually highly contagious. That means these germs can easily spread from person to person when people breathe, cough, sneeze, sing, or even talk, and can make others sick. Doctors suggest these steps to keep you and those around you healthy.

COVER UP: Cough or sneeze into your elbow, sleeve, or a tissue when you are sick. Throw the used tissue in the trash.

STAY HOME IF YOU ARE SICK: Do not go to school or other public places when you are unwell.

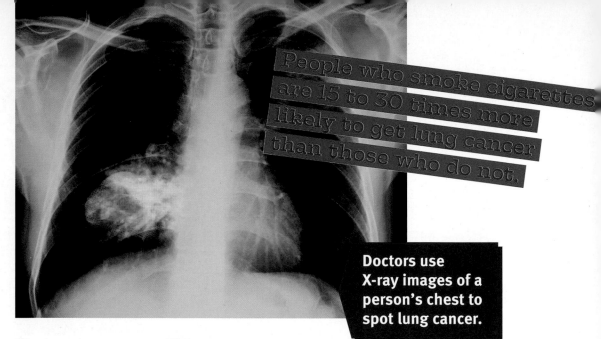

People who smoke cigarettes are 15 to 30 times more likely to get lung cancer than those who do not.

Doctors use X-ray images of a person's chest to spot lung cancer.

Dangerous Disease

Cancer is a disease caused by cells that grow out of control. This can happen in any part of the body, including the lungs. Smoking cigarettes is the number one reason people get lung cancer. To treat this disease, doctors can perform surgery to remove the cancer. Special chemotherapy [kee-moh-THER-uh-pee] medicines can help kill or shrink the cancer too. Targeting cancer with radiation, or beams of energy, can also slow its growth and ability to spread.

Always at Work

You might not give breathing much thought. But every second of every day, your respiratory system is performing this important task. While you sleep, do homework, and play, your lungs never stop. So pause and give your respiratory system a big thank-you. Take a deep breath in. Feel your chest expand. Hear the air rush into your lungs. Then slowly breathe out. AHHH!

Slowly breathing in and out can help relax your body and calm your mind.

Respiratory Care

Doctors, nurses, and respiratory therapists work with us to prevent and treat disease. Here are a few health care professionals who treat the respiratory system, and some of the tests they may perform.

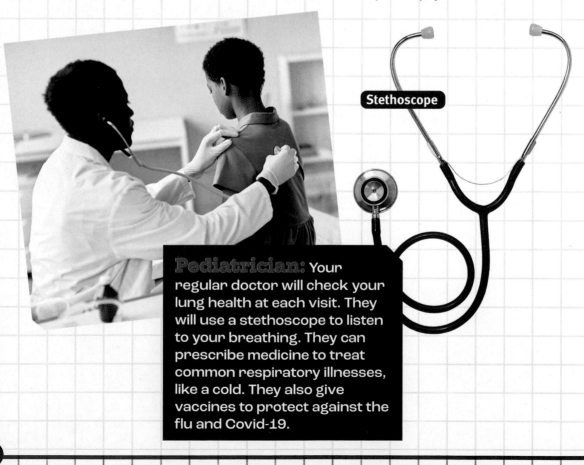

Stethoscope

Pediatrician: Your regular doctor will check your lung health at each visit. They will use a stethoscope to listen to your breathing. They can prescribe medicine to treat common respiratory illnesses, like a cold. They also give vaccines to protect against the flu and Covid-19.

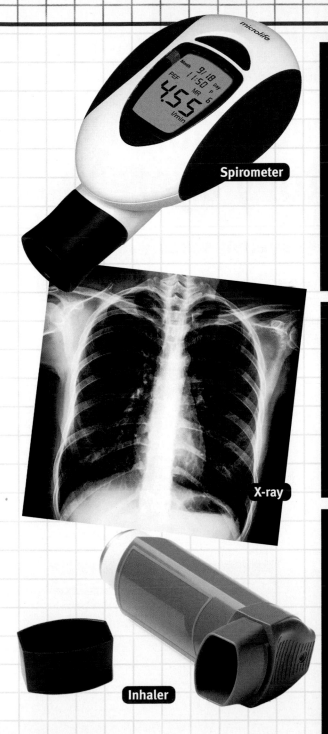

Spirometer

X-ray

Inhaler

Allergist: This doctor treats allergies and asthma. They might have a patient blow into a spirometer [spye-RAH-muh-tuhr] to test lung strength, which can help diagnose asthma. Allergists may place small patches of plant pollens on a person's skin. If their skin turns red, they are allergic to that substance. This doctor can prescribe medicine to treat both asthma and allergies.

Pulmonologist: This doctor helps people with long-term lung issues. A pulmonologist [pul-muh-NAH-luh-jist] might take an X-ray image of a person's chest to look for signs of cancer or pneumonia. Then they will decide how to treat these serious diseases.

Respiratory Therapist: This person helps the patient manage their breathing problem. Some respiratory therapists perform tests to find blockages in the airways or to see if there is difficulty expanding the lungs. Others show patients how best to use an inhaler—a device that delivers medicine that has to be breathed in.

Protect Your Respiratory System

Keeping your respiratory system healthy is important. And if you take care of it now, you will have a healthier future. Here are five things you can do to protect your respiratory health.

Exercise

When you are active, your heart and lungs work harder to supply oxygen to the body. This helps these organs grow stronger.

Avoid Air Pollution

Air pollution includes smoke, dust, and exhaust from cars. Breathing in these substances has been linked to lung problems.

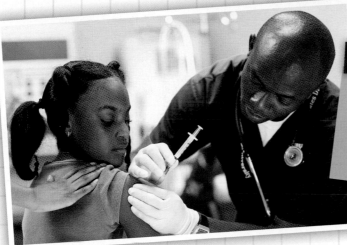

Get Vaccinated

These treatments are available to help prevent lung infections like the flu.

Do Not Smoke or Vape

Fumes from regular cigarettes and e-cigarettes contain chemicals that can damage the lungs.

Eat a Healthy Diet and Drink Plenty of Water

Certain vegetables and fruits contain nutrients, such as beta-carotene and vitamin C, that can boost your immune system and might help protect your lungs from disease. Drinking water helps replace moisture your body loses as you breathe.

True Statistics

The number of people in the world who have asthma: more than 260 million

The combined length of the airways inside your lungs: 1,500 miles (2,400 kilometers)

Speed at which a cough can travel: up to 50 miles per hour (80 km/h)

The number of odors it is thought the human nose can sense: 1 trillion

The weight of an adult's lungs: about 3 pounds (1.4 kilograms), making them the fourth-heaviest organ in the body after the skin, liver, and brain

The amount of air the lungs can hold: 1.6 gallons (6 liters)

Did you find the truth?

F The heart is part of the body's respiratory system.

T A sneeze happens when unwanted particles get into your nose.

Resources

Other books in this series:

 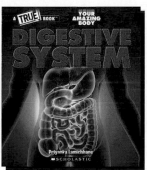 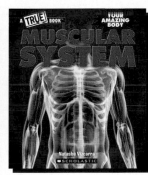 

You can also look at:

Brett, Flora. *Your Respiratory System Works!* North Mankato, MN: Capstone Press, 2015.

Columbo, Luann. *Inside Out: Human Body*. New York: Chartwell Books, 2022.

Ibura, K. *When the World Turned Upside Down*. New York: Scholastic Press, 2022.

Manolis, Kay. *The Respiratory System*. Minnetonka, MN: Bellwether Media, 2016.

Williams, Ben. *Look Inside: Your Heart and Lungs*. Huntington Beach, CA: Teacher Created Materials, 2012.

Glossary

alveoli (al-VEE-uh-lye) tiny air sacs in the lungs

bacteria (bak-TEER-ee-uh) microscopic, single-celled organisms that exist everywhere and that can either be useful or harmful

blood vessels (BLUHD VES-uhlz) any of the tubes in your body through which blood flows

cells (SELZ) the smallest units of an animal or a plant

cilia (SI-lee-uh) tiny hairlike structures attached to some cells

contagious (kuhn-TAY-juhs) likely to spread to and affect others

immune system (i-MYOON SIS-tuhm) the system that protects your body against disease and infection

mucus (MYOO-kuhs) a thick slimy liquid that coats and protects the inside of your mouth, nose, throat, and other breathing passages

organ (OR-guhn) a part of the body, such as the heart or the kidneys, that has a certain purpose

pandemic (pan-DEM-ik) an outbreak of a disease that affects a very large region or the whole world

vaccine (vak-SEEN) a substance containing dead, weakened, or living organisms that causes a person to make antibodies that protect them from the disease produced by the organisms

virus (VYE-ruhs) a very tiny organism that causes diseases

Index

Page numbers in **bold** indicate illustrations.

About the Author

Cody Crane is an award-winning children's writer who specializes in nonfiction. She studied science and environmental journalism at New York University. She always wanted to be a scientist but discovered writing about science was just as fun. She lives in Houston, Texas, with her husband, son, and dog.